I. Introduction

Bond rating agencies have an obvious conflict of interest. They have a financial incentive to accommodate the preferences of bond issuers because they are selected and paid by the issuers. This incentive conflicts with agencies' stated goal of supplying independent and objective credit-risk analysis to investors.[1] Bond rating agencies also have a countervailing incentive to build and protect their reputations for being independent and objective. This paper empirically tests whether rating agency actions systematically vary in a manner which suggests they favor issuer interests – the "conflict of interest hypothesis" – or investor interests – the "reputation hypothesis."

The ongoing string of financial scandals in recent years has highlighted the pervasiveness of conflicts of interest at financial monitors and intermediaries, as well as the fact that these conflicts are not always successfully counterbalanced by reputation-related incentives.[2] The still-accruing evidence indicates that objectivity (and even fiduciary responsibility) has been subjugated to self interest by some accounting firms, equity analysts, corporate officers and board members, stock-exchange specialists, and mutual funds, despite the importance of reputation to franchise value in each of these sectors. Thus, there is an ex ante basis for concern about conflicts of interest at rating agencies, a concern expressed explicitly in recent Congressional legislation and SEC proposals.[3]

Conflicts of interest at rating agencies are important given the fundamental role that

---

[1] This goal is articulated in Moody's (2003), for instance.

[2] In other settings, it has been shown that reputations mitigate moral hazard problems, as in Diamond (1991). Of course, there are also examples of when reputations are ineffective (as in Bulow and Rogoff, 1989).

[3] See, Sarbanes-Oxely Act (2002), SEC (2003).

rating agencies play as delegated monitors in today's capital markets. Most (non-Treasury) debt

securities issued in the U.S. are rated by at least one rating agency, and their importance to

investors, by many accounts, has grown in recent years (see, for instance, Cantor and Packer,

1994, Sinclair, 2003, Fabozzi, 2001, SEC, 2003). In addition, ratings are likely to be particularly

important where the benefits are small, or costs large, to independent credit analysis, such as for

high-grade issuers and asset-backed issuance, respectively. Regulations also rely heavily on

ratings. The SEC designates "Nationally Recognized Statistical Rating Organizations"

(NRSROs), which currently are referenced by at least 8 federal statutes, 47 federal regulations,

and over 100 state laws and regulations.[4]

However, rating agencies have not been formally charged with any illegal activity; and

perhaps there are institutional reasons to expect that their conflicts of interest are well managed.

Certainly rating agencies argue (see, for instance, SEC, 2003, p.23) that safeguarding their

reputation is of "paramount importance." Rating agencies also claim they effectively manage

their conflicts of interest by separating compensation from revenue generation and by

diversifying their revenue base. Conflicts of interest might also be ameliorated by the limited

competition in the ratings industry. With less pressure to compete for fees, rating agencies may

have little incentive to coddle issuers and may instead focus on managing their reputations. Of

course, the degree to which reputation-related incentives keep conflicts of interest in check is an

empirical question.

Our approach to addressing this question is guided by recent criticism of rating agencies,

which has focused on their *delay* in recognizing the credit-quality deterioration of Enron Corp,

prior to its failure at the end of 2001. For example, Zuckerman and Sapsford (2001) summarize:

---

[4] According to the Senate Governmental Affairs Committee report, "Financial Oversight of Enron: The SEC and Private-Sector Watchdogs," October 2002.

"in waiting until Enron's bonds had plummeted in value, the ratings agencies failed in their job of anticipating a company's financial problems and giving investors an early warning." Investor skepticism was heightened by news reports (as in Smith and Zuckerman, 2001) that Moody's, S&P, and Fitch had behind-the-scenes meetings with, and had been lobbied by, executives from Enron, Dynegy, J.P. Morgan Chase, and Citigroup, and "agreed to hold off on making any ratings move," essentially so as not to bankrupt the company. Rating agencies claimed their decision to hold-off on the downgrade was justified, given their belief, at the time, that a pending merger was likely to protect bondholders.

We measure delay as the degree to which ratings changes are anticipated by the bond market, where anticipation is defined as the ratio of an issuer's bond-yield-spread change over the five months preceding the month of the rating change to the total spread change over those five months plus the month of the rating change itself.[5] So, if all of the spread change occurred in the month of the rating change then anticipation would be 0, while if all of the movement occurred in the prior months then anticipation would be 1. By using a monthly frequency, we abstract from delays of only a few days, which is justified by the finding in Holthausen and Leftwich (1985) that the anticipation of rating changes, measured with abnormal equity returns, is large and runs into many months.

Our analysis is novel along a number of dimensions: Our measure of rating change anticipation is new; we are the first to document cross-sectional differences in anticipation and total effects (anticipation plus announcement effects) associated with rating changes; and we are the first to address rating agency conflicts of interest and reputation incentives. We also use a new data set of about 2000 corporate-bond rating changes by Moody's and S&P from 1997 to

---

[5] As discussed later, spreads are calculated relative to other similarly rated and similar maturity corporate bonds.

2002, about twice the size of the data in Holthausen and Leftwich (1985), both in terms of years and number of observations.

We find that downgrades are roughly 75 percent anticipated, but our cross-sectional analysis of anticipation yields no support for the conflict of interest hypothesis. To the contrary, we find substantial evidence consistent with rating agencies protecting their reputations as delegated monitors with timely actions in cases likely to have generated substantial publicity. The results are robust to a variety of controls for other factors that might affect anticipation, such as the size of the downgrade, the size of the total bond-market movement, ratings level, time, industry, having been put on a "watchlist" for a downgrade, and having been downgraded by both firms, as well as to various permutations in the construction of the dependent variable.[6] We also analyze Moody's and S&P rating changes separately. In this analysis, we again find no evidence for the conflict of interest hypothesis, but do find stronger support for the importance of reputation concerns at S&P than at Moody's. We also formulate four additional tests, the results of which also point towards the importance of reputation concerns and away from the conflict of interest hypothesis.

Our findings complement the literature on rating change announcement effects. That literature documents significant announcement effects for downgrades, but not for upgrades, and stronger announcement effects for high-yield downgrades than for investment-grade downgrades.[7] If diminished announcement effects are due to greater anticipation (and we do find greater anticipation for the categories of rating changes found in the literature to have

---

[6] The anticipation measure can be ill behaved when the total effect (the denominator) is small or the anticipation is negative, so we impose restrictions which are varied in the analysis.

[7] See Goh and Ederington (1999), Hand, Holthausen, and Leftwich, (1992), Goh and Ederington (1993), and Holthausen and Leftwich (1985).

insignificant or small announcement effects), our general findings suggest that reputation concerns may help explain differential announcement effects. It is also possible that the diminished announcement effects simply reflect relatively "minor" credit quality events. Consistent with this possibility, we find that total effects are small for the categories of rating changes found in the literature to have insignificant or small announcement effects.

The paper proceeds as follows: Section II formulates the two hypotheses and their testable implications; Section III presents the main results; Section IV addresses robustness, Section V presents additional tests, and Section VI concludes.

II. Hypothesis Development

The incentive for rating agencies to act in the interest of issuers derives from institutional arrangements, whereby issuers pay for issuer-level and bond-level ratings, and also choose which rating agency – possibly more than one – will produce the ratings. Almost all rating agency revenues are from ratings fees. Rating agencies also offer fee-based ancillary consulting-type services to issuers, which may exacerbate conflicts of interest. For example, prior to being issued a public rating, issuers can purchase an "indicative" or private rating, along with "advice" regarding how the company might improve their rating.

Clearly, one mechanism for acting in the interest of issuers is to delay rating downgrades. Delaying the negative news in downgrades may benefit issuers in a number of ways. It postpones the concomitant increase in funding costs. But the benefits may extend well beyond the costs of borrowing, since a downgrade could trigger certain covenants or other conditional obligations. In general, lower rated firms typically must post more collateral and might be treated differently by suppliers – that is, a rating downgrade may have negative feedback effects. In addition a delay gives the firm time, and hence option value, to be able to correct its deterioration in credit quality. This might take the form of detailed discussions with the rating agencies to try to convince them that the downgrade is not warranted, or it might be fundamental changes in capital structure that reduce the firm's leverage and/or enhance its liquidity.

The incentive to delay downgrades may be large in some cases. For example, the incentive to delay downgrades to please issuers may be large when the issuer is a relatively large client, because the fees obtained from issuers are increasing in the number and size of rated bonds. For instance, in addition to an annual fee, Moody's charges between $33,000 and $275,000 *per issue* based on the par value (and complexity) of the issue. The standard per issue fee is calculated as 0.033 percent for the first $500 million of par value and 0.02 percent of additional par value, with a $33,000 minimum and a $275,000 maximum (Moody's 2002).[8]

The delay incentive should also be larger when the downgrade itself is particularly costly to the issuer. One example of a costly rating change is the downgrade from investment-grade to high yield, creating what is commonly referred to as a fallen angel. Financial contracts often contain triggers explicitly tied to this change. For instance, bank-credit lines may be revoked, or derivative contracts may require additional collateral when a firm becomes a fallen angel. In addition, many investors are unable (due to rules and regulations), or unwilling, to hold high-yield securities. This could adversely impact the issuer's ability to access capital markets, adding to the liquidity problems associated with the triggers.

Of course, downgrade delays may be also costly to the reputations of rating agencies. As rating changes become more delayed, investors might find rating agencies less useful as delegated monitors. This gives rating agencies an incentive to be diligent and on top of credit-

---

[8] The rating agencies argue that even the largest issuer provides only a small amount of their total revenue, so this incentive cannot be large. But, of course, that argument does not apply to the incentive to favor an entire class of clients (say all large issuers together).

quality changes. Furthermore, when rating the same issuer, rating agencies may also compete with each other to be perceived as *relatively* timely by investors, and thus the reputation costs of downgrade delays may be enhanced. While multiple ratings can mitigate the conflict of interest via a reputation effect, the custom of multiple ratings could also diminish issuers' leverage over rating agencies.

As evidence that they do not subjugate investors' interests to those of issuers, rating agencies point proudly to their attempts to mitigate the conflict of interest by using fixed fee schedules, rating committees, independent analyst compensation, and other "fire walls" between raters and the collection of revenue. The multitude of measures (as well as their marketing) underscores the reality that the rating agencies must convince investors that ratings are indeed independent, and thus inadvertently emphasizes the seriousness of the incentive to coddle issuers.

The crucial role of reputation to rating agencies implies that they could never completely neglect investor interests. In general, since ratings are widely used by the investment community and rating changes move market prices (we document this later, but it has been well-established by the literature), it appears that the rating agencies have avoided the widespread perception that they serve issuer interests. Even the SEC report to Congress (SEC, 2003, p.23) concluded that "for the most part" market participants believe that the rating agencies have "effectively managed" their conflict of interest. This, perhaps, could be summarized as the view that ratings agencies are generally getting it right.

Rating agencies may also have an incentive to "get it right" faster for some issuers to minimize negative publicity and its consequent reputation cost. Negative publicity, and thus reputation costs, may be increasing when an issuer is a large client and when the downgrade creates a fallen angel, since such cases tend to involve substantial publicity and investor losses.

Empirically, the relative delay for large clients and fallen angels then allows us to identify which incentive is driving the behavior of rating agencies. Evidence that downgrade delays are larger for fallen angels and big clients would suggest that rating agencies are acting in the interest of issuers – support for the "conflict of interest hypothesis." Evidence of smaller downgrade delays for fallen angels and large clients would suggest that rating agencies are primarily acting in the interest of investors to protect their reputations as delegated monitors – support for the "reputation hypothesis."

We measure rating agency delay by the degree to which the bond market anticipates rating changes. There are, of course, a number of other factors that could generate anticipation of rating changes besides intentional delay. For instance, rating agencies will appear slow if they do not respond immediately to gradual changes in credit quality because they only reassess ratings periodically or because ratings move in discrete notches. Second, rating agencies' information advantage over investors may be greater in some cases, or at certain times. Third, there may be other factors relating to the size of the credit quality shock or the firm's initial rating that effect the speed of rating agencies relative to the market. Thus, our main test of these hypotheses, involves regressing the anticipation of a downgrade against variables indicating whether the firm is a large client or a fallen angel, and a variety of controls for other factors that might influence anticipation.

III. Data

We take monthly bond yield and ratings data from Merrill Lynch's bond database. The data, which underlie the widely-followed Merrill Lynch broad corporate bond indexes, includes daily pricing and monthly rating information on over 3000 large, public corporate bonds, from more than 1200 issuers, traded in the US bond market from January 1997 to August 2002. Over

90% of the bonds are issued by firms domiciled in the US, and all the bonds have face value greater than or equal to $100 million and over 1 year in remaining maturity. While on a daily frequency many of the prices will not be from real trades, at a monthly frequency even dealer quotes will be closely tied to the behavior of the individual credit (see Harrison, 2002).

The Merrill Lynch data contains monthly composite bond credit ratings, calculated as the average of the bond's credit rating from Moody's and S&Ps. When the average falls between two ratings, the composite is rounded to the lower rating. This means that the composite rating will tend to capture the first, or "leading edge," downgrade. Composite ratings are updated on the first day of each month to incorporate changes that occurred in the prior month.

To create an issuer-level data set from the bond-level data, we limit the sample to one rating migration per issuer, per month, by selecting the issuer's largest (and, arguably, most liquid and, therefore, best priced) bond when there are multiple bonds migrating within a particular month. We only select migrations with sufficient data to construct yield changes over the six month period ending in the month of the rating change and where there was no rating change within the five months prior to that migration. Prior rating changes could confound the interpretation of our delay measure. For about half the sample, we hand check the migrations data on Bloomberg to confirm that there was no rating actions in the prior 5 months, to alleviate any concern about the composite nature of the ratings, as well as to supplement the data with information on prior "watchlist" assignment and on the identity of which (or both) rating agency changed their rating.

The sample of issuer-level ratings migrations is summarized in Table 1. The sample includes 773 upgrades and 1234 downgrades, all of which took place in the period from July 1, 1997 to July 1, 2002. The greater number of downgrades reflects a substantial increase in the annual pace of downgrades after 1999, as macroeconomic conditions deteriorated.

The original bond-level Merrill Lynch data are also used to create 56 daily "effective" bond-yield-to-maturity indexes, grouped by time-to-maturity and rating. We group the bonds into 7 ratings buckets: AAA, AA, A, BBB, BB, B, and CCC or less. We then take the bonds in each rating group and divide them into 8 maturity buckets.[9] For each sub-bucket, we calculate an average, end of month, bond yield. For each rating change, yield spreads are calculated as the difference between the bond yield at the end of the month (calculated with the first available yield in the subsequent month) and the "appropriate" rating-maturity indexes, based on the bond's rating and maturity in the month prior to the rating change.

IV. Empirical Analysis

1. Total Effect of Rating Changes On Bond Spread Changes

As a prelude to our investigation of delay, we examine bond-spread changes leading up to and through the rating change month. We call this the "total-period" spread change and define it as: $[\text{Spread}_t - \text{Spread}_{t-i}]$), where spreads are calculated monthly at the end of the month, t refers to the month containing the migration month, and i refers to the number of months in the period. We take spreads versus other corporate bonds in order to mimic the change in the credit quality (i.e., default probability or recovery expectation) of that issuer and not market-wide movements that should not show up in ratings, such as cyclical swings, liquidity premiums, and risk premiums.[10]

Table 2a shows the lower quartile, median, and upper quartile of total-period spread

---

[9] Based on whether the maturity is closest to 1, 2, 3, 5, 7, 10, 15, or 20 years. These maturities are chosen to match the maturity of frequently quoted treasury yields.

[10] While rating changes are cyclical, issuers are not downgraded just because the economy weakens.

changes for total periods ranging in length from 1 to 6 months. The table separates downgrades and upgrades, which are then further divided by the issuer's initial and final rating into three categories: high-yield (initial and final rating are both high yield), investment-grade (initial and final rating are both investment grade), and fallen angels (or rising devils, where initial and final rating change category).

The table yields a number of observations. First, consistent with rating changes reflecting credit quality changes, median total period spread changes are greater than zero for downgrades and less than zero for upgrades. Second, the magnitude of the effect varies with the initial and ending rating and is much larger for high-yield firms than for investment grade firms. Apparently a rating change is a bigger credit quality event at lower ratings. Third, the total-period spread changes for downgrades are much larger than for upgrades. This is consistent with the findings in the announcement-effect literature (see, for instance, Hand, Holthausen, and Leftwich, 1992).

Importantly, the results in the table also clearly show that the size of the effect is bigger over a longer window. For example the median total-period spread changes for high-yield downgrades is 390 basis points over a six month total period, but falls to about 80 basis points when calculated over the one month period. The pattern is similar for the other groups. In addition, the inter-quartile ranges narrow as the total-period length narrows. For example, the inter-quartile range for the high-yield downgrade effect is about [25, 1290] with a six month total period, but is only about [-30, 480] with a one month period. Taken together, these last two observations strongly imply that total-period spread changes look more like white noise as the total period narrows, suggesting that bond investors anticipate rating changes months before they occur.[11]

2. Bond Market Anticipation

We attempt to quantify this effect by constructing a measure of bond-market anticipation of rating changes. We define anticipation as the degree to which corporate bond spreads move leading up to the month of the rating change – "prior period spread change" – relative to their movement through the migration month (the "total period" discussed above). More precisely:

Anticipation   = 100 * [Prior Period Spread Change]/ [Total Period Spread Change]

$$= 100 * [\text{Spread}_{t-1} - \text{Spread}_{t-i}]/ [\text{Spread}_{t} - \text{Spread}_{t-i}], \tag{1}$$

where, again, t denotes the month of the rating change and i denotes the number of total months. So, if a rating change is timely, either in the sense that it quickly reflects observable information or reveals new information, this ratio will be close to zero. In contrast, a value near one indicates that the market largely anticipated the rating change.

Measuring anticipation in months is consistent with our findings in the previous section that spread changes are very large in the months before a rating change, as well as with the findings reported by Holthausen and Leftwich (1985) and our view that the monthly frequency is the right one for the costs and benefits of delay to be meaningful to issuers and investors. Using monthly data means we liberally attribute the entire bond spread movement during the month of the rating change to the rating change. This treatment of the timing should have no implications for our cross-sectional regressions.

---

[11] Recall, our spreads are taken to other corporate bonds and so this effect must reflect idiosyncratic anticipation not broad market deterioration.

Table 2b summarizes the anticipation measure across the different groups of rating changes discussed in the previous table. The point estimates in the table confirm that rating changes tend to be mostly anticipated before the month of the rating change. The median anticipations over the six month period range from about 55 percent for fallen angel downgrades, to nearly 85 percent for investment-grade upgrades. The point estimates also show that anticipation decreases with the length of the total period, consistent with the observation from the previous table that total period spread changes become noisier as the total-period length shrinks.

3. Main Results

Our empirical strategy is to regress the anticipation of downgrades on our proxies for intentional delay, controlling for factors which affect anticipation. Our basic specification is:

$$\text{Downgrade Anticipation}_i = \alpha + \beta_1 (\text{Fallen Angel Dummy})_i + \beta_2 (\text{Big Client})_i + \beta_3 (\text{Controls})_i + \epsilon_i \qquad (2)$$

The key variables of interest are the variables "Fallen Angel Dummy" and "Big Client" since these have a differential implication for the conflicts of interest and reputation hypotheses. If rating agencies act in the interest of issuers, β_1 and β_2 should be greater than zero – downgrades of fallen angels and large clients are more anticipated by the market because the agencies have delayed. Conversely, if rating agencies act in the interest of investors to protect their reputations, β_1 and β_2 should be less than zero. We focus on downgrades because that is when the two hypotheses offer opposite predictions for the key variables. A finding of zero for these coefficients would imply that the rating agencies are unbiased.

Table 3a presents results from four different specifications of Equation 2, using a six month event window. The results in this table are all calculated with the following intuitive restrictions on the anticipation measure: We cap anticipation at 100 percent, bound it below at 0 percent, and set it to 100 percent when the total period spread change is less than 20 basis points. Conceptually, 100 and 0 percent are natural bounds for the anticipation measure. In addition, when the denominator (i.e., the total spread change) is small or negative one might reasonably infer that the rating change was fully anticipated and was reflected in bond spreads *before* the total period. So, in these instances we set anticipation to its maximum. Robustness with respect to various restrictions on the anticipation measure is presented after the discussion of our main results.

The first specification in Table 3a includes the fallen angel dummy variable, the log of the number of bonds an issuer has outstanding (our first proxy for "large client"), and a dummy variable indicating if the initial rating is high-yield. The results, shown in column 1, indicate that fallen angels are 20 percentage points less anticipated by the bond market than other investment-grade downgrades (the omitted rating category), and that downgrades of firms with 1 percent more bonds outstanding are 5 percent less anticipated. The rating agencies appear more timely at changing ratings in cases when the downgrades are likely to generate substantial publicity, which we interpret as evidence for the reputation hypothesis and against the conflict of interest hypothesis. The coefficient on the high-yield dummy is -18, which is consistent with riskier downgrades generally being less anticipated by the bond market.

The next specifications show that the evidence in favor of the reputation hypothesis is robust to additional controls. Moreover, because the estimated coefficients on the control variables have the "expected" signs, they buttress our interpretation of the left-hand-side variable as a measure of anticipation. The first of these additional specifications, shown in column 2, augments the stripped-down specification with three control variables: the magnitude of the rating change, the total period bond-spread change, and the square of the total period bond-spread change. The coefficients are all significant at the 5 percent level. The coefficient on the fallen angel dummy and the log of the number of bonds are again negative, but a bit smaller in absolute size than in the first specification. The coefficients on the control variables indicate that downgrades are 12 percent less anticipated when the issuer's original rating is high-yield, 3 percent less anticipated when they occur over 1 additional rating notch, and 3 percent less anticipated for every 1 percentage point (100 basis point) increase in the total-period spread change. The coefficient on the square of the total-period change is close to zero. The negative relationship between downgrade anticipation and the size of the total period spread change, as well as the rating notch variable, may reflect the fact that our anticipation measure is constructed from bond *yields*, which are convex functions of bond *default risk*.

The next specification tests robustness to replacing the log of the number of bonds with the log of the issuer's total par value of outstanding bonds. As shown in column 3, downgrades are about 3 percent less anticipated when an issuer has 1 percent more outstanding bonds. The point estimate is significant at the 5 percent level. The other coefficients and their statistical significance are essentially identical to those in the previous specification. The results are also immaterially different, as shown in column 4, when quarterly-time-dummy variables and industry-dummy variables are included. F tests, not shown, indicate that the quarterly dummies are statistically different from 0, but the industry dummies are not.

Table 3b addresses the robustness to alternative restrictions on the anticipation measure and the sample. All specifications in the table use the full list of control variables used in the last specification of the previous table. The table first considers robustness to using a longer-term (1 year) measure of anticipation. Given the requirement that the migration not be preceded by another migration during the total period, the longer-term delay measure reduces the sample size from 1234 to 809 downgrades. Nevertheless, as shown in the first column, the qualitative results are the same as in the previous table. The size of all the coefficient estimates are smaller, but still statistically significant at the five percent level – again, except the industry dummies.

The second specification (column 2) uses the six-month anticipation measure, but drops the restriction that all downgrades not be preceded by other rating changes in the total period, which increases the sample size to 1772 rating downgrades. The coefficient estimates and their significance levels are very close to the results in the previous table.

Next, we change the definition of a trivial spread change – the cut off below which the downgrade is assumed to have been anticipated – from 20 basis points to 10 basis points. As shown in the third column, this reduces the magnitude of the coefficient on the fallen angel dummy and the log of the number of bonds a bit, but again the results are very similar. As another alternative, we drop the observations with negative total period spread changes, rather than assume, as we did, that such observations imply 100 percent anticipation. As shown in column 4, the results are again similar, except the coefficient on the fallen angel dummy jumps to -21.

The last specification, the results for which are shown in column 5, drops all restrictions relating to the anticipation measure. This yields a regression with almost no explanatory power, indicating that the intuitive restrictions on the anticipation measure are important. However, the consistency of the results to various alternative restrictions indicates that the results do not depend on the precise way in which the restrictions are imposed.

4. Anticipation Analysis by Rating Agency

While the majority of our analysis is conducted on our sample of composite rating migrations, we conduct analysis of Moody's and S&P downgrades separately to look for differential effects. The test for the conflict of interest versus the reputation hypothesis is the same as in the previous tables. However, we also add a control for whether the firm was put on "watch" for a downgrade during the total period, as well as a dummy variable indicating whether the downgrade by one rating agency was affirmed by a downgrade from the other rating agency. Clearly being put on the watch list is expected to increase anticipation. The expected impact of a downgrade affirmation is less clear. However, to the extent that a downgrade affirmation implies a larger event, one would expect less anticipation, as we have already shown that larger events generate less anticipation independently of delay. Because they were hand collected only for downgrades with total-period spread changes greater than 20 basis points, the sample is reduced to 372 Moody's downgrades and 358 Standard and Poor's downgrades.

The results for the Moody's sample, displayed in Table 3c, point in the direction of the reputation hypothesis, but are somewhat weaker than those obtained using the composite ratings. In all three specifications, the coefficients on the fallen angel dummies are not significant, but the coefficients on the "Big Client" proxies are still negative and significant – two at the 5 percent level and one at the 10 percent level. The coefficients on the two new variables in specifications without the quarterly and time dummy variables, shown in the first two columns, indicate that downgrades are 7 percentage points more anticipated when the firm is put on watch for a downgrade in the prior period, and 8 percentage points less anticipated when both rating agencies downgrade the firm in the migration month. When quarterly and time dummies are added, as shown in the third column, coefficients on the two new variables are somewhat smaller than in the first two specifications and insignificantly different from zero.

The results for the S&P regressions, shown in Table 3d, point more strongly in the direction of the reputation hypothesis. The coefficients on the fallen angel dummy variables, shown in columns 1-3, are all about -19, and significant at the 5 percent level, and the coefficients on the client size proxies are negative, with all but one significant at the 10 percent level. The other coefficients are similar to those in the Moody's regressions. Putting a firm on watch for a downgrade leads to between 7 and 10 percentage points more anticipation, and having been downgraded by both rating agencies tends to coincide with between 4 and 8 percentage points less anticipation.

In both the Moody's and S&P regressions, the positive impact on anticipation of the watch list is intuitive, and the negative impact of "double agency" downgrades is consistent with the previously discussed result that larger downgrades tend to coincide with less anticipation. One difference with the results in Table 3a is that the total period spread change is no longer significant, although if we combine the Moody's and Standard and Poor's samples (not shown) the coefficient on the total period spread change is again significant and negative.

V. Additional Results

1. Upgrades versus Downgrade Delays

The conflict of interest hypothesis predicts that rating agencies would delay downgrades and perhaps hasten upgrades, since downgrades delays benefit issuers. The reputation hypothesis predicts rating agencies might be more timely with downgrades, since downgrades may generate more publicity than upgrades. Thus the conflict of interest hypothesis would predict that downgrades are more anticipated by the bond market than upgrades, while the reputation hypothesis would predict the opposite. To test this implication, we combine our sample of downgrades with upgrades, and regress:[12]

Anticipation $_i$ = α + β_1 (Upgrade vs. Downgrade)$_i$ + β_2 (Controls)$_i$ + ϵ_i (3)

The results, summarized in Table 4, again point towards the reputation hypothesis. As shown in the first column, in a stripped down specification with only a constant and a dummy variable for whether the rating change is an upgrade, we find that upgrades are 10 percent more anticipated than downgrades. The result is significant at the 5 percent confidence level. Adding our usual list of controls, along with a dummy variable for whether the rating change creates a rising devil (upgrade from high-yield to investment-grade), weakens the result to a still statistically significant 7 percent, as shown in the second column.

2. Is Reputation Only A Post-Enron Concern?

Soon after Enron defaulted towards the end of 2001, criticism of rating agencies peaked. To test whether reputation concerns at rating agencies were a response to this criticism, and thus only a recent concern among rating agencies, we split the sample into a pre-2002 period and a post-2001 period and re-run the regressions in Equation 2. However, as the results in Table 5 show, the evidence is actually stronger for the reputation hypothesis pre-Enron. In the early sample period, the coefficient on the fallen angel dummy variable is -22, the coefficient on the log of the number of bonds is -4, and both are statistically significant at the five percent level. In the post-2001 period, the coefficient on the log of the number of bonds is -5 and significant at the 10 percent level, but the coefficient on the fallen angle dummy is insignificantly different

---

[12] Analogous restrictions on the anticipation measure for upgrades are made.

from zero. The limited evidence of the reputation hypothesis in the later period could be due to the difficulty in identifying significance with the smaller sample size (203 observations) relative to the earlier period (1031 observations). It is also possible that the bond market may have become more diligent in the post-Enron period. Regardless, the results suggest that the importance of reputation concerns is not a post-Enron phenomenon.

3. Downgrade Propensity

One potential concern is that our methodology only considers downgrades that actually occur, so our test would fail to detect conflicts of interest that manifest in favored clients not being downgraded at all. To explore this possibility, we expand our sample and then test whether the probability of an issuer being downgraded in a particular month is negatively related to being a "Big Client," after controlling for other factors that are likely to affect the probability of a downgraded.

The new sample contains 32,983 monthly issuer-level observations. The dependent variable is a dummy variable for whether the issuer has been downgraded in that month. Our independent variable of interest is, as above, the "Big Client" proxy (either the log of the number of bonds or a dummy variable for whether the issuer has greater than the upper quartile number of bonds). The controls include a variable for the initial rating at the beginning of a six month total period, the prior-period spread change from t-6 to t-1, and an interaction between the high-yield dummy and the five month prior-period spread change. The model is estimated with a Probit specification:

$$\text{Downgrade}_{i,t} = \alpha + \beta_1 (\text{Big Client})_{i,t} + \beta_2 (\text{Prior Spread Change})_{i,t} + \beta_3 (\text{Controls})_{i,t} + \epsilon_{i,t} \quad (4)$$

The results from the model, shown in Table 6, once again point towards the reputation hypothesis. As shown in the first column, which reports marginal effects and standard errors, a one percent increase in the number of bonds leads to a 0.3 percent increase in the likelihood of a downgrade. The result is significant at the 5 percent level. The marginal effects for the control variables are as expected. High-yield issuers are more likely to be downgraded, issuers with large prior-period bond spread changes are more likely to be downgraded, but the effect is mitigated if they are high-yield (i.e., the marginal effect on the interaction term is negative). This last result is consistent with the greater gap in credit quality between rating notches at the lower-end of the credit quality spectrum. The second specification replaces the log of the number of bonds variable with a dummy variable for whether the issuer has more than the upper quartile number of bonds. The marginal effect, shown in the second column, indicates that large firms defined in this way our .5 percent more likely to be downgraded, controlling for other factors. The marginal effects and their significance are the same as in the previous specification.

4. Anticipation and Opacity

Our results could potentially be biased due to the omission of controls for issuer opacity, although the direction with which opacity effects anticipation is ambiguous. On the one hand, opacity may make it more difficult for ratings agencies to evaluate firms, and thus opacity ceteris paribus would increase rating agency delays (in the spirit of Morgan, 2002, who shows that rating agencies disagree more when there is more opaqueness). On the other hand, opacity creates more scope for ratings agencies to have an informational advantage over investors and thus opacity would decrease delays. We address this question in Table 7 by adding new controls to Equation 2 for firm opacity. The opacity proxies are a variety of balance-sheet measures from Compustat: the ratio of tangible assets to total assets, the ratio of income taxes paid to total assets, the ratio of dividends paid to total assets, the ratio of goodwill to total assets, total assets, the ratio of current assets to current liabilities, the ratio of total debt to total assets, and the ratio of interest expense to operating income. None of the controls are significant, either singly or jointly, suggesting that anticipation and delay are not strongly tied to issuer complexity (at least after controlling for other variables, such as rating and spread change). Because of the need to merge with Compustat, however, the sample size is significantly reduced. Regardless, the evidence for the reputation hypothesis remains quite robust in all four specifications.

VI. Conclusion

In conclusion, our analysis indicates that the bond market anticipates rating changes, but we find no evidence consistent with rating agencies acting in the interests of issuers due to a conflict of interest. Instead, rating agencies appear to be relatively responsive to reputation concerns and so protect the interests of investors. Of course, our analysis is not a comprehensive test of rating agency behavior. Conflicts of interest may manifest in ways we do not test, such as biased rating levels. Moreover, our results only show what is statistically discernable, on average, and thus can not rule out the possibility that in some instances rating agencies have acted in the interest of issuers. A final caveat is that our measure of anticipation—constructed with monthly data—cannot discern delays of a few days.

References:

Bulow, Jeremy and Kenneth Rogoff, 1989, "Sovereign Debt: Is to Forgive to Forget?" *American Economic Review*, 79, 43-50.

Cantor, Richard and Frank Packer, 1994, "The Credit Rating Industry," *Quarterly Review*, Federal Reserve Bank of New York, 19, 1-26.

Diamond, Douglas W., 1991, "Monitoring and Reputation: The Choice Between Bank Loans and Directly Placed Debt," *Journal of Political Economy*, 99, 689-721.

Fabozzi, Frank J., ed., 2001, *The Handbook of Fixed Income Securities*, 6th Edition, McGraw Hill: NY.

Goh, Jeremy C. and Louis H. Ederington, 1993, "Is a Bond Rating Downgrade Bad News, Good News, or No News for Stockholders," *Journal of Finance*, 48, 2001-8.

Goh, Jeremy C. and Louis H. Ederington, 1999, "Cross-Sectional Variation in the Stock Market Reaction to Bond Rating Changes," *Quarterly Review of Economics and Finance*, 39, 101-12.

Hand, John R. M., Holthausen, Robert W., and Leftwich, Richard W., 1992, "The Effect of Bond Rating Agency Announcements on Bond and Stock Prices," *Journal of Finance*, 47, 733-52.

Harrison, Paul, 2002, "The Impact of Market Liquidity in Times of Stress on Corporate Bond Issuance," in *Proceedings of the Third Joint Central Bank Research Conference on Risk Measurement and Systemic Risk*. Basel: Bank for International Settlements.

Holthausen, Robert W. and Richard W. Leftwich, 1985, "The Effect of Bond Rating Changes on Common Stock Prices," *Journal of Financial Economics*, 17, 57-89.

Moody's Investor Service, 2002, "Moody's Debt and Preferred Stock Rating Fee Schedule," November 2002.

Moody's Investor Service, 2003, "The Role and Function of Rating Agencies: Evolving Perceptions and the Implications for Regulatory Oversight," February 2003.

Morgan, Donald P., 2002, "Rating Banks: Risk and Uncertainty in an Opaque Industry," *American Economic Review*, 92, 874-888.

The Securities and Exchange Commission, 2003, "Report on the Role and Function of Credit Rating Agencies in the Operation of the Securities Markets," January 2003.

The Senate Governmental Affairs Committee, 2002, "Financial Oversight of Enron: The SEC and Private-Sector Watchdogs," United States Senate, October 2002.

Sinclair, Timothy J., 2003, "Bond Rating Agencies," *New Political Economy*, 8, 147-161.

Smith, Rebecca and Gregory Zuckerman, "Enron, Dynegy Work to Salvage Merger Deal," *The Wall Street Journal*, November 28, 2001, page A3.

Zuckerman, Gregory and Jathon Sapsford, "Why Credit Agencies Didn't Switch Off Enron – S&P Cries 'Junk,' But the Warning Comes Too Late," *The Wall Street Journal*, November 29, 2001, page C1.

TABLE 1: RATING CHANGES
By Year and Rating

	UPGRADES			
	Investment Grade -> Investment Grade	High Yield -> Investment Grade	High Yield -> High Yield	Total
1997	45	6	29	80
1998	90	11	66	167
1999	76	13	62	151
2000	90	12	59	161
2001	82	12	65	159
2002	20	5	30	55
Total	403	59	311	773

	DOWNGRADES			
	Investment Grade -> Investment Grade	Investment Grade -> High Yield	High Yield -> High Yield	Total
1997	27	3	19	49
1998	96	15	71	182
1999	86	19	121	226
2000	90	10	102	202
2001	152	19	201	372
2002	84	13	106	203
Total	535	79	620	1234

TABLE 2a: Total Effect Of Rating Changes On Bond-Spread Changes

Bond-Spreads are the bond's option adjusted yield to maturity relative to corporate bond-yield indexes with similar rating and maturity as the bond experiencing the rating change. The length of the total period is the number of months leading up to and going through the end of the month of the rating change. *High yield* refers to those rating changes for which the bond's rating is below BBB- before and after the rating change. *Investment grade* refers to migrations for which the bond's rating is above BB+ both before and after the rating change. *Fallen angels* refers to those rating changes for which the bond's rating is investment grade before the raitng change and high-yield after. *Rising devils* refers to the opposite case.

Total-Period Bond-Spread Changes (Basis Points)

	Downgrades				Upgrades			
High yield **Length of total period (months)**	#	Lower Quartile	Median	Upper Quartile	#	Lower Quartile	Median	Upper Quartile
1	620	-26	81	479	311	-54	-7	29
2	620	-23	143	697	311	-80	-18	24
3	620	-13	214	892	311	-85	-15	33
4	620	4	272	995	311	-112	-35	30
5	620	1	332	1258	311	-151	-40	30
6	620	25	390	1292	311	-170	-49	32
Fallen Angels and Rising Devils **Length of total period (months)**								
1	79	-9	21	155	59	-58	-15	12
2	79	-6	47	158	59	-70	-22	7
3	79	0	79	177	59	-76	-26	6
4	79	-4	90	171	59	-122	-35	2
5	79	10	98	172	59	-138	-51	-9
6	79	-1	101	195	59	-145	-68	-1
Investment Grade **Length of total period (months)**								
1	535	-5	3	17	403	-9	-1	7
2	535	-6	6	31	403	-13	-1	9
3	535	-7	9	39	403	-17	-2	11
4	535	-7	11	48	403	-23	-5	8
5	535	-7	12	51	403	-28	-5	10
6	535	-8	14	57	403	-28	-7	11

TABLE 2b: Bond Market Anticipation

Bond-yield spreads are calculated as in the previous panel. *Anticipation* refers to the bond-spread change over the prior period relative to the bond spread change over the total period, where the prior and total periods begin some number of months before the migration, the prior period ends at the beginning of the migration month, and the total period goes through the migration month.

Anticipation (percent)

	Downgrades		Upgrades	
	#	Median	#	Median
High Yield				
Length of total period (months)				
1	--	--	--	--
2	620	33	311	39
3	620	52	311	66
4	620	61	311	79
5	620	64	311	80
6	620	67	311	84
Fallen Angels and Rising devils				
Length of total period (months)				
1	--	--	--	--
2	79	17	59	29
3	79	47	59	54
4	79	60	59	69
5	79	56	59	70
6	79	58	59	83
Investment Grade				
Length of total period (months)				
1	--	--	--	--
2	535	44	403	43
3	535	63	403	60
4	535	69	403	73
5	535	74	403	81
6	535	77	403	83

TABLE 3a: Evidence For Reputation Hypothesis: Downgrade Anticipation Regressions

The construction of the dependent variable is as follows: The event window is the 6 months leading up to and through the end of the rating change month; the raw anticipation measure is the bond spread change over the first five months of the total period expressed as a percent of the bond spread change over the entire total period; anticipation is capped at 100 percent and bounded below at zero; when the bond spread change over the total period is less than 20 basis points, anticipation is set at 100 percent. *High yield* refers to an indicator variable for whether the initial rating is lower than BBB-. *Fallen angel* refers to an indicator variable for whether the downgrade changes the bond's status from investment-grade to high-yield. *Number of bonds* and *Total par value* refer, respectively, to the issuer's number and total par value of bonds outstanding. *Magnitude of rating change* refers to the number of notches over which a migration occurred. *Total-period spread change* refers to the bond spread change over the six month total period. Industry dummy groups are banking and finance, basic industry, capital goods, communications and media, consumer goods, energy and utility, and services (the omitted category). Coefficient standard errors are reported in parentheses.

Independent Variables	(1)	(2)	(3)	(4)
Constant	89**	91**	106**	95**
	(1.77)	(2.08)	(5.92)	(4.40)
Fallen angel	-20**	-16**	-16**	-16**
	(3.92)	(3.99)	(3.99)	(4.02)
Log(number of bonds)	-5**	-4**	--	-4**
	(1.20)	(1.17)		(1.19)
Log(total par value)	--	--	-3**	--
			(0.87)	
High yield	-18**	-12**	-12**	-12**
	(2.03)	(2.08)	(2.11)	(2.15)
Magnitude of rating change	--	-3**	-3**	-3**
		(1.05)	(1.05)	(1.05)
Total-period spread change	--	-1**	-1**	-1**
		(0.08)	(0.08)	(0.08)
Total-period spread change squared	--	0**	0**	0**
		(0.00)	(0.00)	(0.00)
Quarterly dummies	No	No	No	Yes
Industry dummies	No	No	No	Yes
# of Observations	1234	1234	1234	1234
R^2	6.58%	12.49%	12.45%	15.14%
F-Test	<0.0001	<0.0001	<0.0001	<0.0001

* indicates significance at the 10% level
** indicates significance at the 5% level

TABLE 3b: Robustness of Evidence For Repuation Concerns:
Additional Downgrade Anticipation Regressions

The dependent variable is anticipation. Independent variables are defined as in the previous panel, and coefficient standard errors are reported in parentheses. Column numbers identify new dependent variable restrictions and sample construction. Specifically:
(1) Anticipation is calculated using a 12 month event window.
(2) The sampling restriction that rating chnages are not preceded by ratings changes in the previous six months is dropped.
(3) The assumption that when the total period spread change is less than 20 basis points, anticipation is 100 percent is replaced with the assumption that when the total period spread change is less than 10 basis points, anticipation is 100 percent.
(4) Observations with total period spread change less than 0 are dropped.
(5) All restrictions on the raw anticipation measure are dropped.

Independent Variables	(1)	(2)	(3)	(4)	(5)
Constant	93**	93**	90**	88**	-59
	(5.51)	(3.64)	(4.58)	(5.70)	(51.68)
Fallen angel	-9**	-16**	-12**	-21**	19
	(4.51)	(3.36)	(4.19)	(5.08)	(47.27)
LOG(number of bonds)	-3**	-2**	-3**	-3**	8
	(1.42)	(0.95)	(1.24)	(1.47)	(14.00)
High yield	-5*	-9**	-8**	-16**	32
	(2.61)	(1.77)	(2.24)	(2.85)	(25.28)
Magnitude of rating change	-2*	-3**	-3**	-3**	-14
	(1.13)	(0.91)	(1.10)	(1.31)	(12.39)
Total-period spread change	-1**	0**	-1**	0**	-1
	(0.10)	(0.05)	(0.08)	(0.10)	(0.95)
Total-period spread change squared	0**	0**	1**	0**	0
	(0.00)	(0.00)	(0.00)	(0.00)	(0.00)
Quarterly dummy variables	Yes	Yes	Yes	Yes	Yes
Industry dummy variables	Yes	Yes	Yes	Yes	Yes
# of Observations	809	1772	1234	891	1234
R^2	13.55%	12.20%	12.13%	12.02%	2.69
F-Test	<0.0001	<0.0001	<0.0001	<0.0001	0.4135

* indicates significance at the 10% level
** indicates significance at the 5% level

TABLE 3c: Evidence Of Reputaton Concerns At Moody's:
Downgrade Anticipation Regressions

The construction of the dependent variable assumes a six month total period. The sample is defined as downgrades by Moody's that are not preceded by another rating change from either rating agency in the five months leading up to the downgrade, and that coincide with at least a 20 basis point total-period spread change. *Watch list* refers to a dummy variable for whether an issuer was put on watch for a downgrade in the five months leading up to the downgrade month. *Moody's and S&P downgrade* refers to a dummy variable for whether both Moody's and Standard and Poor's downgraded the firm in the migration month. The other independent variables are defined as in the previous panels Coefficient standard errors are reported in parentheses.

Independent Variables	(1)	(2)	(3)
Constant	69**	84**	65**
	(5.17)	(12.16)	(9.53)
Fallen angel	-1	-2	0
	(6.98)	(7.01)	(7.09)
Log(number of bonds)	-5**	--	-5**
	(2.37)		(2.45)
Log(total par value)	--	-3*	--
		(1.73)	
High yield	-8	-7	-8
	(5.05)	(5.13)	(5.21)
Watch List	7*	7*	5
	(3.83)	(3.88)	(4.03)
Moody's and S&P downgrade	-8*	-8**	-4
	(4.03)	(4.04)	(4.18)
Magnitude of rating change	-1	-1	-2
	(2.07)	(2.08)	(2.09)
Total-period spread change	0	0	0
	(0.29)	(0.29)	(0.31)
Total-period spread change squared	0	0	0
	(0.00)	(0.00)	(0.00)
Quarterly dummy variables	No	No	Yes
Industry dummy variables	No	No	Yes
# of Observations	372	372	372
R^2	5.97%	5.46%	15.84%
F-Test	0.0040	0.0085	0.0032

* indicates significance at the 10% level
** indicates significance at the 5% level

TABLE 3d: Evidence Of Reputaton Concerns At Standard and Poor's:
Downgrade Anticipation Regressions

The construction of the dependent variable assumes a six month event window. The sample is defined as downgrades by Standard and Poor's that are not preceded by another rating change from either rating agency in the five months leading up to the downgrade, and that coincide with at least a 20 basis point total-period spread change. Independent variables are defined as in the previous panels. Coefficient standard errors are reported in parentheses.

Independent Variables	(1)	(2)	(3)
Constant	71**	85**	70**
	(5.19)	(12.44)	(11.97)
Fallen angel	-19**	-19**	-18**
	(8.06)	(8.09)	(8.34)
Log(number of bonds)	-5*	--	-5*
	(2.47)		(2.61)
Log(total par value)	--	-3	--
		(1.80)	
High yield	-9*	-8	-10*
	(5.00)	(5.04)	(5.21)
Watch list	9**	10**	7*
	(3.86)	(3.90)	(3.92)
Moody's and S&P downgrade	-7*	-7*	-6
	(3.99)	(3.99)	(4.28)
Magnitude of rating change	-2	-2	-3*
	(1.74)	(1.75)	(1.78)
Total-period spread change	0	0	0
	(0.18)	(0.18)	(0.19)
Total-period spread change squared	0	0	0
	(0.00)	(0.00)	(0.00)
Quarterly dummy variables	No	No	Yes
Industry dummy variables	No	No	Yes
# of Observations	358	358	358
R^2	7.19%	6.89%	15.59%
F-Test	0.0009	0.0015	0.0052

* indicates significance at the 10% level
** indicates significance at the 5% level

TABLE 4: Additional Evidence For Reputation Hypothesis:
Test of Upgrade Relative to Downgrade Anticipation

The construction of the dependent variable is as follows: The event window is the 6 months leading up to and through the end of the rating change month; the raw anticipation measure is the bond spread change over the first five months of the total period expressed as a percent of the bond spread change over the entire total period; anticipation is capped at 100 percent and bounded below at zero; when the bond spread change over the total period is less than 20 basis points, anticipation is set at 100 percent. *Upgrade* refers to a dummy variable for whether the rating change is an upgrade. *High yield* refers to an indicator variable for whether the initial rating is lower than BBB-. *Fallen angel* refers to a dummy variable for whether the rating change is a downgrade and also changes the bond's status from investment grade to high yield. *Risen devil* refers to a dummy variable for whether the rating chnage is an upgrade and also changes the bond's status from high yield to investment grade *Number of bonds* refers to the issuer's number of bonds outstanding. *Total-period spread change* refers to the absolute value of the total period spread change. *Magnitude of rating change* refers to the number of notches over which a migration occurred. Industry dummy groups are banking and finance, basic industry, capital goods, communications and media, consumer goods, energy and utility, and services (the omitted category). Coefficient standard errors are reported in parentheses.

Independent Variables	(1)	(2)
Constant	76**	91**
	(0.90)	(3.51)
Upgrade	10**	7**
	(1.45)	(1.53)
Fallen angel	--	-7*
		(3.71)
Risen devil	--	-19**
		(4.26)
High yield	--	-11**
		(1.61)
Number of bonds	--	-2**
		(0.86)
Magnitude of rating change	--	-1
		(0.72)
Total-period spread change	--	-1**
		(0.08)
Total-period spread change squared	--	0**
		(0.00)
Quarterly dummy variables	No	Yes
Industry dummy variables	No	Yes
# of Observations	2007	2007
R^2	2.18%	12.33%
F-Test	<0.0001	<0.0001

* indicates significance at the 10% level
** indicates significance at the 5% level

TABLE 5: Is Reputation Only A Post-Enron Concern?

The construction of the dependent variable is as follows: The event window is the 6 months leading up to and through the end of the rating change month; the raw anticipation measure is the bond spread change over the first five months of the total period expressed as a percent of the bond spread change over the total period; anticipation is capped at 100 percent and bounded below at zero; when the bond spread change over the total period is less than 20 basis points, anticipation is set at 100 percent. *High yield* refers to an indicator variable for whether the initial rating is lower than BBB-. *Fallen angel* refers to an indicator variable for whether the downgrade changes the bond's status from investment-grade to junk. *Log(number of bonds)* and *Log(total par value)* refer, respectively, to the issuer's number and total par value of bonds outstanding. *Magnitude of rating change* refers to the number of notches over which a migration occurred. *Total-period spread change* refers to the bond spread change over the six month total period. Industry dummy groups are banking and finance, basic industry, capital goods, communications and media, consumer goods, energy and utility, and services (the omitted category). Coefficient standard errors are reported in parentheses.

| Independent Variables | DOWNGRADES | |
	(1) 1997-2001	(2) 2002
Constant	89**	86**
	(4.17)	(8.55)
Fallen angel	-21**	5
	(4.42)	(9.84)
Log(number of bonds)	-4**	-4*
	(1.33)	(2.65)
High yield	-13**	-2
	(2.38)	(5.39)
Magnitude of rating change	-2**	-2
	(1.11)	(3.62)
Total period spread change	-1**	-1**
	(0.10)	(0.22)
Total period spread change squared	0**	0**
	(0.00)	(0.00)
Quarterly dummy variables	Yes	Yes
Industry dummy variables	No	Yes
# of Observations	1031	203
R^2	13.01%	17.99%
F-Test	<0.0001	0.0121

* indicates significance at the 10% level
** indicates significance at the 5% level

TABLE 6: THE PROBABILITY OF MIGRATION

The dependent variable is a dummy variable for whether the issuer has been downgraded in month t. *Number of bonds* refers to the number of bonds outstanding for an issuer in month t. *High-yield (t-6)* refers to a dummy variable for whether the initial rating at the beginning of a six month total period is greater than BBB-. *Prior-period spread change* refers to the yield spread change from t-6 to t-1. The model is estimated as a probit specification. Sandard errors for the marginal effects are reported in parentheses.

Independent Variables	DOWNGRADED IN MONTH t Marginal Effects in Percent	
	(1)	(2)
Constant	-4.5**	-4.4**
	(0.08)	(0.07)
High yield (t - 6)	1.7**	1.6**
	(0.07)	(0.07)
Log(number of bonds)	0.3**	--
	(0.04)	
Greater than upper quartile number of bonds	--	0.5**
		(0.06)
Prior-period spread change	0.3**	0.3**
	(0.04)	(0.04)
High yield (t - 6) * Prior-period spread change	-0.3**	-0.3**
	(0.04)	(0.04)
# of observations	32983	32983
Log likelihood	-5118	-5131
Significance	(0.00)	(0.00)

* indicates significance at the 10% level
** indicates significance at the 5% level

TABLE 7: OPACITY AND DELAY

The construction of the dependent variable is as follows: The event window is the 6 months leading up to and through the end of the rating change month; the raw anticipation measure is the bond spread change over the first five months of the total period expressed as a percent of the bond spread change over the entire total period; anticipation is capped at 100 percent and bounded below at zero; when the bond spread change over the total period is less than 20 basis points, anticipation is set at 100 percent. *High yield* refers to an indicator variable for whether the initial rating is lower than BBB-. *Fallen angel* refers to an indicator variable for whether the downgrade changes the bond's status from investment-grade to high-yield. *Number of bonds* and *Total par value* refer, respectively, to the issuer's number and total par value of bonds outstanding. *Magnitude of rating change* refers to the number of notches over which a migration occurred. *Total-period spread change* refers to the bond spread change over the six month total period. All models include quarterly and time dummies (not reported). Industry dummy groups are banking and finance, basic industry, capital goods, communications and media, consumer goods, energy and utility, and services (the omitted category). Coefficient standard errors are reported in parentheses.

Independent Variables	DOWNGRADES			
	(1)	(2)	(3)	(4)
Constant	86**	78**	66**	80**
	(6.70)	(12.14)	(11.60)	(12.53)
Fallen Angel	-8	-9*	--	-9
	(5.24)	(5.35)		(5.44)
LOG(number of bonds)	-5**	-5**		-5**
	(1.81)	(1.84)		(1.89)
High yield	-8**	-9**		-9**
	(3.29)	(3.59)		(3.87)
Magnitude of rating change	-1	-1	--	-1
	(1.73)	(1.73)		(1.74)
Total-period spread change	-1**	-1**	-1**	-1**
	(0.22)	(0.23)	(0.22)	(0.23)
Total-period spread change squared	0**	0**	0**	0**
	(0.00)	(0.00)	(0.00)	(0.00)
Tangible assets/total assets	--	8	9	8
		(10.81)	(10.85)	(10.91)
Income taxes paid/total assets	--	-32	17	-31
		(97.63)	(95.18)	(98.29)
Dividends paid/total assets	--	-8079	271	-8499
		(9543.70)	(9164.60)	(9768.10)
Goodwill/total assets	--	17	19	17
		(13.68)	(13.72)	(13.81)
Total assets	--	--	--	0
				(0.00)
Current assets/current liabilities	--	--	--	0
				(2.00)
Total debt/total assets	--	--	--	-1
				(4.82)
Interest expense/operating income	--	--	--	0
				(0.56)
# of Observations	555	555	555	555
R^2	14.21%	14.64%	12.64%	14.75%
F-Test	<0.0001	<0.0001	<0.0001	<0.0001

* indicates significance at the 10% level
** indicates significance at the 5% level